CAPE TOWN

A VISUAL SOUVENIR

Struik Publishers (Pty) Ltd
(a member of the Struik Publishing Group)
80 McKenzie Street
Cape Town 8001
Reg. No.: 54/00965/07

ISBN 1 86872 027 6

Copyright in published edition:
Struik Publishers (Pty) Ltd 1997
Copyright in text: Struik Publishers (Pty) Ltd 1997
Copyright in photographs: Alain Proust with the
exception of the following:
Erhardt Thiel/SIL: pp36–37, Mathew Cargill p58;
Nigel Dennis/SIL: p75; Hein von Hörsten/SIL: pp56, 57;
Lanz von Hörsten/SIL: pp44, 63; CLB/SIL: p80;
Mark Skinner/SIL: p20.

Managing editor: Annlerie van Rooyen
Designer: Janice Evans
Text: Thea Coetzee and Anouska Good

Reproduction: cmyk pre-press
Printing: Times Offset (M) Sdn Bhd

*TITLE PAGE   The yachts Eye of the Wind and Spirit
of Victoria at the Victoria and Alfred Waterfront.*

RIGHT   Boats at sunset, Kommetjie.

INTRODUCTION

Cradled between the ocean and the mountains, the bustling city of Cape Town pulses with life. Flower sellers and other informal traders, peddling their wares with noisy good humour, are a familiar sight in the heart of the city while, down at the harbour, the Victoria and Alfred Waterfront complex attracts millions of visitors every year.

But Cape Town has a quiet side as well: it is home to some of the world's most beautiful beaches, enticing visitors with their clean white sand and sparkling waters. Tranquillity can also be found in the Cape of Good Hope Nature Reserve, the lush Constantia Valley and Kirstenbosch Botanic Gardens, serene oases in an otherwise teeming cosmopolitan city.

LEFT Klein Constantia Estate produces internationally recognised wines, winners of numerous awards.

TABLE MOUNTAIN

Standing guard over Cape Town, Table Mountain, at 1 086 metres above sea level, is one of the best-known landmarks in the world. Its cableway takes visitors on an exhilarating ride to the top, from where they are treated to a breathtaking view of the entire peninsula. For the more energetic, several hiking trails climb its slopes.

Sculpted from sandstone, Table Mountain supports a wide variety of fynbos (a floral kingdom unique to the region), as well as abundant birdlife and fauna. The famous 'tablecloth' of cloud, which heralds the strong winds of Cape Town's notorious southeaster, is a familiar sight in summer.

LEFT Table Mountain, flanked by Devil's Peak, Lion's Head and Signal Hill, provides a spectacular backdrop to Cape Town.

ABOVE *An aerial view of the Cape Peninsula showing Devil's Peak to the left of Table Mountain, Lion's Head to the right, and Signal Hill in the foreground.*

ABOVE Table Bay and Robben Island seen from the air with Signal Hill, Lion's Head and Table Mountain in the foreground.

FOLLOWING PAGES Looking towards Cape Point from the top of Table Mountain.

PREVIOUS PAGES Table Mountain at sunset as seen from Rietvlei near Milnerton.
ABOVE AND OPPOSITE Once a prison and now a tourist attraction, Robben Island
lies within sight of Table Mountain.

CITY CENTRE

Cape Town's central business district boasts numerous attractions. The Company's Gardens, site of the Houses of Parliament and the South African Museum, is a microcosm of Cape history. Also offering a glimpse into the region's past is the Bo-Kaap, or Malay Quarter, with its many colourful houses and mosques situated on the slopes of Signal Hill.

For entertainment, the city is crammed with pubs, restaurants, night clubs and shops. And for people-watching, nothing can compare with the fleamarket at Greenmarket Square. The stalls, manned by some rather colourful characters, display all manner of wares, from clothing, books and jewellery to some of the most interesting bric-a-brac to be found.

LEFT The world-famous Mount Nelson Hotel, where visitors to Cape Town come to be pampered in gracious colonial style.

ABOVE *The Company's Gardens.*

OPPOSITE *The fleamarket at Greenmarket Square.*

OPPOSITE The imposing Renaissance-style City Hall in the late evening.

TOP LEFT AND ABOVE The city shrouded in mist.

ABOVE AND OPPOSITE Cape Town's architecture is a heady mixture of old and new, contributing to the cosmopolitan character of the city.

OPPOSITE Cape Town's famous Coon Carnival enlivens the city streets each year when they celebrate the new year.

TOP LEFT AND ABOVE The cheerful faces of flower sellers and stall holders at Cape Town's markets.
FOLLOWING PAGES Picturesque houses in the Bo-Kaap, or Malay Quarter.

THE WATERFRONT

A shopper's paradise and entertainment mecca, the Victoria and Alfred Waterfront is a favourite destination of visitors to South Africa. The huge shopping centres contain a host of specialist boutiques and informal traders and there are also countless restaurants and pubs, a bustling food market, a cinema complex, and a world-class aquarium, to name but a few of the attractions.

Visitors can take a harbour cruise, attend a concert in the open-air amphitheatre, watch the activties of the working harbour or just stroll around enjoying the musical offerings of the numerous buskers.

LEFT The Victoria and Alfred Waterfront with the old Port Captain's Building on the left.

FOLLOWING PAGES The Waterfront with Table Mountain's 'tablecloth' in the background.

PREVIOUS PAGES   The Waterfront overlooking Table Bay, with Robben Island on the horizon.

LEFT   The imposing QE2, docked in Cape Town's harbour.

FOLLOWING PAGES   The lights of the Victoria and Alfred Waterfront beckon visitors at night.

ATLANTIC
SEABOARD

*E*xtending from Table Bay to Cape Point, the Atlantic coast is the epitome of scenic splendour. With the mountain range known as the Twelve Apostles creating a spectacular setting, this stretch of coastline is blessed with some of the Cape's most glorious beaches.

Clifton is where the sun-worshippers can be found, while Llandudno is known for its millionnaires' mansions and unspoilt beach. Further south lies the village of Hout Bay, curved around an enchanting, sheltered harbour. From here, the scenic Chapman's Peak Drive twists and turns its way along the dramatic coast until reaching its end at Noordhoek.

LEFT The chilly waters of the Atlantic Ocean wash the shores of Sea Point, with its throng of high-rise buildings in the background.

FOLLOWING PAGES An aerial view of Sea Point.

PREVIOUS PAGES *The Twelve Apostles form an impressive backdrop to the Atlantic coast.*

LEFT *Clifton beach, favourite haunt of the Cape's sun-seekers.*

ABOVE AND OPPOSITE *Popular beaches interspersed with small tranquil bays are a feature of the Atlantic seaboard, as can be seen from the coastline around Llandudno.*

FOLLOWING PAGES Leopard Rock overlooks the sparkling waters of Hout Bay.

RIGHT Hout Bay harbour, with Chapman's Peak Drive in the background.

FOLLOWING PAGES Chapman's Peak, one of the most spectacular drives in the country.

CAPE POINT

A rocky outcrop at the southern-most tip of the Cape Peninsula, Cape Point is known for the magnificence of its scenery and the abundant variety of its flora. However, the Cape of Good Hope Nature Reserve was originally proclaimed as a safe haven for the endangered bonte-bok and Cape mountain zebra, as well as the unique chacma baboon.

Both the restaurant and old lighthouse offer views out over the often turbulent seas that can only be described as awesome. The marine life of the region includes dolphins, seals and whales and, on a calm day, the waters of the area are ideal for diving, with the wrecks of Smitswinkel Bay being a major attraction.

LEFT The beautiful beach at Smitswinkel Bay is the jewel of the Cape of Good Hope Nature Reserve.

ABOVE *The easy way to the top of Kanonkop, Cape Point.*

OPPOSITE *The lighthouse at Cape Point.*

FALSE BAY

False Bay is known for its lovely sandy beaches. As the water temperature here is considerably warmer than that of the Atlantic coastline, these beaches are ideal for swimming. However, False Bay is also noted for the gale force winds which, according to legend, were responsible for the mysterious 'disappearance' of the Dutch vessel the *Flying Dutchman* in 1600.

Muizenberg beach is a popular spot for family holidays, but nearby St James is still the quiet village where Cecil John Rhodes retired. To the south lie Kalk Bay, a charming fishing town, and Simon's Town, steeped in naval history. A lovely way to enjoy the False Bay scenery is to take the train from Cape Town to Simon's Town.

LEFT These brightly coloured beach huts are the trademark of the beach at St James.

FOLLOWING PAGES Jackass penguins at Boulders beach near Simon's Town.

ABOVE A view of the harbour at Simon's Town.

ABOVE *Fish Hoek is popular with boating
enthusiasts and is the site of several regattas.*

FOLLOWING PAGES *Waves break over the
harbour wall at Kalk Bay.*

CAPE WINELANDS

Groot Constantia, with its handsome Cape Dutch homestead, was built by governor Simon van der Stel in the seventeenth century. The first wine of the Cape was produced there and today, it is still the major attraction of the Cape Peninsula wine route. The homestead is filled with many treasures, including beautiful period furniture and works of art. Groot Constantia boasts two very good restaurants, a wine museum and daily tours of the cellars. The world-famous wines can be bought on the estate.

Other wine estates forming part of the Cape Peninsula wine route are Steenberg, Klein Constania, and Buitenverwachting. The restaurant at Buitenverwachting is well known for its excellent cuisine.

LEFT The Manor House at Groot Constantia, pride of the South African wine industry.

PREVIOUS PAGES *A panoramic view of the vineyards at Klein Constantia.*

LEFT *Buitenverwachting, one of Cape Town's premier wine estates.*

KIRSTENBOSCH AND SURROUNDS

Kirstenbosch, the headquarters of the National Botanical Institute of South Africa, was once part of Cecil John Rhodes' Groote Schuur Estate. Today it provides a fit setting for the Cape's indigenous flora with a particular feature being the fragrant garden specially designed for the enjoyment of the blind. During the hot summer months open-air concerts are held on Kirstenbosch's lawns.

Also situated on the slopes of Devil's Peak is the University of Cape Town, the oldest university in Africa. The nearby Rhodes Memorial, designed by Herbert Baker, affords a magnificent view of the city and visitors can enjoy its excellent restaurant and tea garden, as well as several good walking trails.

LEFT The lush slopes of Kirstenbosch support a wealth of botanic riches.

ABOVE, TOP RIGHT AND OPPOSITE *Beautiful strelitzias, red disas and proteas flourish at Kirstenbosch.*

ABOVE AND OPPOSITE Leafy hideaways create pleasant places in which to relax while enjoying a stroll through the Gardens.

LEFT *The University of Cape Town, with Jameson Hall as its focal point.*

FOLLOWING PAGES *An aerial view of Rhodes Memorial.*

ENDPAPERS *False Bay at dawn.*